W9-CKH-269

Windy Place

WINDY PLACE

Henry Blakely

bp

BROADSIDE PRESS

12651 Old Mill Place   Detroit, Michigan 48238

Copyright ©1974 by Henry Blakely
All Rights Reserved
First Edition
First Printing

No part of this book can be copied, reproduced,
or used in any way without written permission
from Broadside Press, 12651 Old Mill Place,
Detroit, Michigan 48238

ISBN: 0-910296-14-6 Cloth $6.00
ISBN: 0-910296-15-4 Paper $2.50
LCN:

Manufactured in the U.S.A.

Acknowledgments

CRISIS, October 1940 . . . . "Dread Automaton"

VOICES, Winter 1950 . . . . "Earthworm"

Contents

Introduction

Henry Blakely's poetry is notable for an ordered sorrow—and for a distinct perception of the *dis*ordered bread, brick and embroideries of man-at-large.

Perhaps he will be called by many "The Poet of Sixty-Third Street." He has said, in recounting over and over again, almost lovingly, the adventures and vagaries of Sixty-Third Street, "You will think I never leave there." We get to know Club Arden, which became a vacant lot. We leap over time and see the tavern wall graffiti. We know Lucy, Club Arden's queen, who, after "making it" through shakedowns, showups/all the Sixty-Third Street weather, finally "split the scene/and went to hell and felt at home." Even so, her creator decides, "she tarries/and is sweet." We meet Sixty-Third Street pigeons who, "too tired for flight," move "slow/ with glassy eye," are "mashed by wheels," and "lie/like smashed gray hats/in bits of silence"—reminding their observer of old men on that Street, "moving slow, with glassy eye."

"Woodlawn 1972" is akin. Henry Blakely sees "the killed houses," "littered streets/from which/*even*" (my italics) "the Blacks have fled."

In this book may be found, also, salutes to heroes, romantic songs, tributes to the varying voices and faces of nature. There are those involvements with destiny and high relevance and neoned message often to be found in a sensitive poet's first book.

And there is Henry Blakely's masterpiece, "My Daddy." A little epic.

Henry Blakely never cared to rush into print. Many subscribers to poetry will be grateful that he has decided to share, at last, the figures of his landscape.

—Gwendolyn Brooks
Chicago, May 1974

9

I

My Daddy

My Daddy died age sixty-seven,
one Saturday night,
hale at nine,
gone at eleven.

Tall for his time,
my Daddy,
and quick and lean
as men must be when
lithe and alive
and on the move.

"Came in and took a bath,"
they said.
"And then went out."
And that was that.

In rare remembered times
he magicked some,
on special evenings
making nuts and candies come
into his hand from out the air.

Daddy knew things. He knew
beyonds, why air collapsed
a can in which the steam
had turned to water,
words—how to spell them,

fractions, ratios,
who was who in the paper
read each evening.
Men listened
when Daddy spoke.

And on his burying day,
her voice near to surprise,
"He was so mighty,"
Mother said.

Mother was earth
and nourished us.
But Daddy saw earth
as mire
trapping the feet and movement
and promises of far journeys.

But yet he paused
to touch my mother
and I became,
and Julius and Edgar.
And after that
he never really got away.

Maybe we were weight and tether,
a circumstance of ugly weather.
Maybe loss and need conspired
to make him love us.
Maybe he was going nowhere
and we
were not detour at all.

Sometimes we'd wrestle on the floor.
The three of us
would try to hold an arm down.
We never could.

I was given Daddy's name.
Strange,
seeing it on the funeral directory
made time bunch up,

rubbèd out the little space
separating him from me
and for a moment let me know
how it was to be dead.

Daddy made things. It was delight
having his opinions on clocks
and skate-wheel scooters and airplanes
and boats to sail in the bathtub.
Lindbergh
had just made aeroplanes real.

And when Daddy died,
a barbecue grille,
his own invention,
"That did everything but buy the meat"
was not finished.
Howard kept it for a time.
But tin and steel do not endure
like stone.

Daddy was going to a party
when he died,
his date too young for me.
She was there at the funeral,
and Gracie was there,
and Helen, Howard's mother.

"I'll leave if you cry,"
I told my mother.
But I don't think I would have.
I was upset by them being there.
Never out loud had we spoken of them.
And then there they all were—
in the same room.

North from Atlanta and hunger,
Daddy had come to Chicago
when he and this century
were young together,

and met my mother
also fleeing
a barrens in Kentucky.

In Mother's eyes were mirrored
meadowlands and vineyards,
and roads without exhausting lengths
or dusts,
and houses somehow white.
So when at last
I came to Georgetown
I did not know the place.

Nor did I know
where in Atlanta Daddy lived.
I never knew his people,
except Aunt Gertrude
who married a gambler
and did well.

Charlie and Sally
were grandparents never seen.
"Sally was a bitch,"
Aunt Gertrude said.

Daddy did not look age sixty-seven
as he lay there,
neat as always,
still large and lifelike,
his high yellow
not quite a pallor,
freckles, dimpled chin,
hair not gray.
The young look
would have pleased him.
He would have said, "Good job"
to the undertaker.
Some woman cried;
not my mother:
we had warned her.

Daddy made a cap once
with ropes in it
to press against his hair
and urge it wavy.
Mother called him a fool.
And once
when he came home wearing bangs,
she waited until he slept
and cut them off, and said,
"No fool like an old fool."
Mother never understood
how truth could kill a man.

But she loved Daddy,
and Aunt Mary
called *her* a fool,
and Aunt Martha
shook her head.

They were Mother's sisters.
Mother heard them in most things.
But not about Daddy.
Went to Detroit
to him
when we were grown,
kicked Helen out.
Or maybe it was more than that,
or maybe less,
old guilts, old debts,
old memories,
or love again that didn't last.

"Grow old," my Mother said,
not seeing that Daddy feared to die
and felt that death could not come
if he was up and moving on.

Daddy was his own man,
no clocks, nor gate, nor stall.
He bowed later though, when tired.

We moved a lot.
Bills weren't met.
Mother cleaned and cried
in each old house come to
and felt she paid too much
for Daddy's dreams.

And broke a plate glass window once
in the hand laundry
Daddy had set up,
hammered holes
in the plasterboard walls
and then went screaming out the door
to hide behind a tree
and we behind her
one, two, three.

And there were whispers
of times in jail for nonsupport.
Daddy, it was said,
learned Steamfitting there.

Hunger I came to not care for,
nor for Daddy,
before I was old enough to see
that dreams
must be paid for,
that it is as right
to want fuel for flight
as for boiling beans.

"He was the learned one,"
Aunt Gertrude said,
speaking of Daddy's hegira
to Chicago where the streets were,
paved and wide.

Nine, ten, and eleven,
we three,
when Daddy left to live with Helen,
and Howard was born.

I remember him, hesitant
in the basement doorway.
"Our summer homes" Mother once joked
of basements,
telling a neighbor we tried
to be on first or second floors
above the ice in winter.

Hesitant he stood and I
the older. Something in him
saying goodbye.

I told him
if he did not want us,
nobody did.
And years later, a man,
and in Detroit,
he did not know me.
He said once, in my presence,
"My son," but he talked to Howard,
not to me.

Burial was on a working day,
attendance small,
and speakers fished
for things to say.
The box was closed.

But still he lived
in each of us. Howard
his image, lean, and feral, kind of.
In Edgar
the back of Daddy's head and neck
touched with elan a stocky body.
And Edgar
talked to machines
like Daddy did.
Julius wore his strength for women
and breathed his dreams
and hatred of clocked time.

I had his name,
his cleft chin,
and not in as great measure, perhaps,
the other things.

From each of us, his sons,
parts could have come
to make him whole again.

Strange now
that I remember him kindly,
see him
as more right than wrong.
Strange now
that I see Mother wanting bread,
needing it—for us,
and know that bread
was not enough.

Or maybe
not so strange.
With all the facts not gathered in,
he lies awry beneath the neat
and there is straightening
to be done.

I think the earthworm
knows when it is summer

II

Autumn Perspective

Henry Blakely's beard
is gray.
When did this happen?
Yesterday
he was a boy
and times to come
were wind and wine.

Where are the winds
and wines,
the girls
and melodies?
What journeying
is tracked in this gray?
What knowing
of orbits, cities,
penicillin, atoms?
What knowing
there are no girls
anymore,
but only women,
co-predators
in the fierce land?

What knowing
"This can be happening to me."
And death is possible,
even wise?

Lucy

Club Arden is a vacant lot
where Lucy shook it, lush and hot,
as does her shade now,
like as not.

Graffiti on the tavern's walls
depicted Lucy
kindly,
holding her men, talking
her talk, greeting
mostly with love the good scene,
the mostly beautiful people.
And, time to buy, she took her turn
and downed her glass each trip around.

Graffiti, caves, and ancient man.
Did either they or Lucy plan
to tell to time
how each ran?

Lucy never rolled a drunk.
She did not jive,
she gave
all that was paid for,
used, was used, useful,
making it through shakedowns, showups,
all the Sixty-third Street weather,
till finally she split the scene
and went to hell and felt at home.

Graffiti leaving, but no concrete
ritualed by the Lucy feet.
Yet she tarries
and is sweet.

On Sixty-Third

On Sixty-third
the pigeons fly
and roost on El track
or store-front eave.
And in each spring
the old ones die.

Too tired for flight,
and moving slow
with glassy eye
until
mashed by wheels,
they lie
like smashed gray hats
in bits of silence
from which
there sometimes gleams
a broken blood
red like ragged ribbon
or, still and slow,
a glassy eye.

On Sixty-third
the old men die,
moving slow
with glassy eye.

The Pale One

He comes, the Pale One,
meat-eater odor in his sweat. He comes
with his gods and his guns to subdue us.

His priests and armies trample our fields;
he comes to kill our men.
His gunboats thunder in our rivers;
he comes to capture our women.
His wings roar in our skies like locusts;
he comes to enslave our children.

Truth means War to him.
Peace means War to him.
The giving and taking in love
means War to him.

He comes, the Pale One,
man-stalker, looter; his young teethe on wartoys;
he comes to subdue us.

Weapon yourselves, my Brothers.
Rise and strike the Pale One,
the maker of death and desert.

To Where
Are Stars Before Us

Not absolute the now chiefs of men,
not eternal their writs, interdicts.
Let them be in neither love nor hate
as we move to the rim of the world

seeing for ourselves the universe
beyond their thin white ring around us.
That pale men are invincible
is false, a fiction told at fires dim

in dim forests, needful to creatures
knowing of time and impermanence.
Let us unchain ourselves—examine—
oust—gods, costumes, idea, whatever

enslaves. Let us cease being strident,
substancing the loud lie with loud scream.
Let us move to where the firmament
begins, to where are stars before us.

Sambanjo

Blind old Sam
and his steel-string banjo
merging to make music
at Thirty-ninth and State,
brown and resonant
and ivory Sambanjo,
early and lean
and lithe and late.

Why do you sing, Sambanjo?
Are you sorry for the people?

Near the center
of the city, strings and
fingers shaping ditty
loud like shrieking brakeshoes
and slither-soft
like courtway muggers.
Sing Chicago town, Chicago.
Sing our song, Sambanjo.

Sing loud for us the tumult
of an el train's
castanets
in clackety-clack
high on its track.
Sing sweet for our brown women
weed and flower sweet.
Sing sad for our downed houses.

Why do you sigh, Sambanjo?
Are you sorry for the people? ·

Sing languaged hips,
legs nyloned, lush,
wares and buyers
in five dollar rooms.
Sing of this town of tavern
and temple,

of puddle and parkland,
of meat and barebone, Sambanjo.

Sing. Sing of sun and paean
where stink perfumes.
Hometown, whoretown,
V.D. Rosie
pretty on the boulevards,
hit-town, clout-town,
even in the citadels.
Sing our song, Sambanjo.

Sing our parade. Sing our charade.
Sing. Sing our mute
no-color Mardi Gras,
our cops and square johns,
our pushers and prosties,
our broken-down people.
Sing moon-moan. Sing sun-gone.
Sing Chicago town, Chicago.

Why do you sob, Sambanjo?
Are you sorry for the people?

Mating Song
Not for Young Lovers

(On reading *The Naked Ape*)

I have been programmed to love you,
to see
in your cheeks, your cheeked buttocks.
You have no up or down, no
hind or fore.
You, palindrome, mnemonic
entity,
are trysting place for sperm and egg,
nothing more.

Your either-end tastes and smells of
the salt sea.
Your mucuses are sea-stuff.
But your twice-twinned hemispheres
are made for love,
are hind and fore indeed,
raising
my blood timed to sea-tide, and so
I love you.

Our Stubborn
and Determined Rose

Our stubborn and determined rose
doesn't care that winter's come
or that frost has etched each petal
with ice and age.

Each petal center is still deep yellow,
as in summer.

No bees applauding, no aphids sucking
allow our rose reason to stay,
giving a moment longer of rose.

There were twelve once.
Some never bloomed.

Prone our rose should be, its reaching ended,
time pressing it to amalgam with
the maker-dust.

But a stem still straight supports
our stubborn rose. It endures,
perhaps with rose awareness,
and lengthens summer.

Man

Some thing once stood
upon a hill
and bade us move
without our will,
and made us man.

A protozoan
is man,
a sense of sun
struggling from selfmuck
to cellwalls one's own.

A vertebra
is man,
mindless, but knowing
of life, spine angled always
toward the light.

A dreaming ape
is man,
now and then pausing
to mate and continue,
now and then pausing
to find the dawn marvelous.

An artificer
is man,
a gods-and-weapons-maker,
tomb-builder, time-dweller
in yesterday and tomorrow.

An idea
is man,
weftage of all the heritage,
all the forgotten stagings,
all the linking and ongoing.

An awakening
is man.

But waking
has driven away
the dream. Rockets wing
where angels were.
We can die now.
No thing stands awesome
on a hill
and bids
"Be man."

The Johnsons

The Johnsons' rooms have yellow walls
and dimmer-switches and hardwood floors.
The house is squat and close to home.

They built the place from plans they made
and greened their yards and squared them round
to make a nest for evenings come.

The place was near the edge of town.
New neighbors built, land values rose.
"I'm glad we settled early here,
now couldn't afford it," Jim Johnson said.
Some love, some fear, and life went by;
the children came and grew, were gone.

The Johnsons stayed to tend their yards
and walk their rooms with yellow walls
and wait for final evenings come
to house so squat and close to home.

Sunny Morning

I walked out one sunny morning,
saw the world and it was good,
a bird, a squirrel, a green tree,
even in October.

Earthworm

I think the earthworm
knows when it is summer.
And in summer
that is the thing to know.
We cannot affirm this
but neither can we deny it.
He moves in directions and numbers
not seen in winter.
There are no mounds of yellow earth
piled high in the snow.

And yet
the generations of earthworms move.
The creatures sense their mission
and accomplish it
without formal statement of law,
without science or art,
and, seemingly, without awe.

Woodlawn 1972

How sad
is old Aristes
when passing through
these littered streets
from which
even the Blacks have fled.

How sad,
seeing the killed houses,
the cairns and empty places
where once bouzoukis musicked,
where lamb
was sacrifice for feast
and dark red wines
rose wine and dark through spirits
as laurel leaves through air.

Even I
am sad. Even I,
Black,
and with no memory
of these places
when they were young.

Benjamin Elijah

The words, the monuments,
a grateful people raise
to Benjamin Elijah Mays
will stand
as markers in time
and the land.

But those markers will not be for him.
Heroes are their own way.
The markers will be for us
who wander less sure,
have no North Star to follow.

The markers will make known to us
and to the years,
Benjamin Elijah journeying
to show where hand-holds were
on the mountain steep and smooth.

The markers will tell to us,
and to other men,
how he was lone,
far forward in the hostile land
when we
could not cover him,
when we
were not organized for sortie,
or march.

And when other men
sing of their heroes
we will know to speak our brother's name,
argue for his admittance
into the pantheon.

Enemies are enemies not always
because they hate us
but because
they love their own.

The markers will remind us.
We love our own.
Our heroes will no more be nameless
and forgotten
because we did not record them,
sing of them.
We know now.
What goes forward
into tomorrow,
into time,
is not what the hero does
but what the legend sings.

The markers will be our song,
our memory of Benjamin Elijah
sung loud
so that time
will not dim him,
so that he
will not die.

Be you my season of delight
and I will neither question why
nor search for purpose in the sky.

III

Morning Song

I do not need a springtime,
or place apart, to love you.
I need no cloak of night, no starmoon
silvered on a sea.

I love you in the rain, and when
we're washing dishes after supper.
I love you moving, sleeping, talking.
You being, I love.

Music you are and mostly
bright May weather. I love you
twice the numbered sands of deserts
and lengths of beaches.

Come, Let Us Be Love Together

Come, let us be love together.
Let us be living and laughing together.
And when
your senses say no more when
I am near,
let us lie down together
and be dust together.

Not Forever

Not forever will we love.
Not forever will we move.
So let us on this unmarked eve
kisses give
and be alive.

When I Think of You

When I think of you
I think of heather
and you a maiden on it
and we together.

And yet I know that there's
no heather in your past,
nor in the land you left on coming here.
And you have not been maiden
for some twenty year.
And we are not together,
oh, my dear.

But still I think of heather
when I think of you.
My love, my fairest maiden,
forever young and new.

Perfume Is

Perfume is
when it smells like you.
Clothes are beautiful
when you wear them.
It is wonderful to sleep beside you,
knowing the dream is real,
to wake with my hand touching you,
my heart pounding unsayable things.
Oh, my dear, you are good.
I adore you.

Constantly

Constantly you are with me.
The night heat
And next day's afterglow
Are equal reality
And indistinguishable sweet.

How Can I Say?

How can I say, my love, that you
are food and fire to me?
How breathe to you a poem
the rude feet of words
crush and make awry,
my love?

Look into me and sense the things
I cannot say. Look into me
and sense the void
I would be, were you not,
and so, no lilt of singing
in my day.

Winter warms, it is near to spring
and men and song will say
it is a time
for greening, for roads sunward.
But I will say your name,
and be glad.

Trial

When you return
you will be spring to me
and to my life again will come
deep green of leaf and love
ripening into summer.

Time moves slowly
while I ache for you.
Pack your things and come on home.

When you return
as fallow earth, as leaf,
as ripened wheat returns,
each in its season.

The miles are long
and I am wanting you.
Catch that plane and come on home.

When you return
I will pirouette
to the musics of merry weather
for gone, gone will be
all the wide seas, gone,
and you near to me.

I am old
when we are lone apart.
Come to me. Be with me.

Love Needs No Lyric Summer

Love needs no lyric summer
nor synthetic spring.
Love is its own season,
its own song.

Green Comb

Love wears a green comb in her hair
and brings me pretty things to eat
on rapid, flannel-slippered feet.

Stir

What stirs me stirred ancient men,
not earth nor love is new.
Why then do I marvel
that there should be a you.

Neither are you winged,
and Lady, you are clay.
Why then do I fear
that you will fly away?

I say you are not marvelous,
say fruit so sweet has rind.
But my heart sings of summer
above the winter mind.

Three Songs

My words that say
I love you
are flights unwinged,
unmelody.
Words have not harpsound
nor soft wind.

Believe I feel I love you.
Believe I soar
with music in my heart
and harpsound in my mind.

* * *

My day does not begin with sunrise.
My day begins when some message comes
to tell me you are in the world
alive and well.

Nor does sunset bring the dark.
Dark comes when your door closes,
you on one side,
me on the other.

* * *

A poet
sang of his lady
and now, dust,
she does not die.
Why do I sing of you,
sweet dust to be?
Ask why
did the poet sing.
Ask why.

Programmed with birdlores,
high, the earth is a ball below,
the bombers home on stars
and do not swoop to kill like eagles.

IV

Manimal

On feet of wind
his bombers run
and deaths are soon
and hard and deep.
Manimal's effusion
scums the sun
and stills the seas
and lakes to sleep.

Manimal, machined
and neat of claw,
kills even his own,
even when, bellies up,
they sue for truce
per ancient law.
Manimal kills brother,
bitch, and pup.

Cain was no fable
and time
may not come again
to Spring.

Automaton

The dread automaton passed here today.
His huge misshape hid the sun.
Beneath his iron feet beauty died
and vibrant life oozed redly out
through crushing fingers of steel.
Bird song,
sky song,
music of wind and water,
against the booming cadence
of his voice,
trilled to nothing.

6 June

A fair June day,
but not to Pierre
was the June day fair.
War had blown the world away
and left him standing there.

In 1943 the bodies of hundreds of Polish officers,
massacred in 1940-41, were exhumed at Katyn Forest.
Whether the slayers were Russian or German has not
yet at this time thirty years later been determined.

Katyn Forest

A forest. September.
The morning is redgreen. Ragged
men with indelible faces
bend
and sounds of spading
scrape the air.

Metal voices
strive to prop chaos
in rectangles
of order. Shovels drop.
The ragged men align along
the new-dug pits and turn
to face the East,
and the guns.

Twenty meters forward
outlines of other men
are dark
against an apocalypse sun
early and barely above
treetops whose shadow and green are
red with sun-color.
A breeze stirs tunics, neat,
not yet frayed by velocities
of time and wind.

Fingers steel
to deliver steel. Guns
rehearse old angry arias.
The ragged anonymous men

do not hear and start
as in surprise, or
sway slow when bullets ransack,
spill most secret stuffs
from secret places and
hurl the ragged men
to lie nameless
in heaps and ancient oneness
with the earth.

Quick claps of sound
rebound
from the horizons
and then move out again
in rings beyond the things
that made them.
The men, nameless, emptied,
cut from time's cord,
do not move.
The sun is red. Red flecks
the grass still green,
the new-turned yellow earth.

Again
the metal voices
make metal sounds occur
as mags are cleared and weapons shouldered.
The pits are filled.
The regal guns, victorious,
move away, and their soldier court
moves with hollow eye.
A coiled and acrid air is lonely
where ragged men once stood.

We dug these pits, peopled them
with death.
We have exhumed you. We
are not proud.
The wind moves over you
and sickens us.

The wind plays with you, examines
your rags.
Worms salvage our society.
These pits are impasse
to our science.
These are September days,
end of man's summer.

'Nam

Joe went to a soldier's rest,
a pound of honor on his chest.

And Death Is Our Desire

The air relays the beat of hammers swung
and whirling lathes weave planes and tanks and guns
and finished hulls are floated off the runs
down to the sea. The songs of war are sung
by men of every place and race and tongue.
For it is true that Nature's warring sons
were digging, molding, forging, iron tons
when time was new, and stars were new and young.

And peace is hunger conjured in the mind,
a sense of half-fulfilled and promised things,
a bird that falls in wind from fledgling wings.

Sound the hammer loud and heap the fire.
And blow the muted bugle for our kind.
Our goal is death, and death is our desire.

Song for Missionaries, Mercenaries, Merchants, and Other Slavers

With ball ammunition
load and lock
load and lock your pieces.

Brothers! we bring them liberty
and self-determination.
Let the temple bells ring out
this day of their salvation.

Cut off the hands of all the men
and civilize the women.
Who wants his bastard children reared
by creatures dark and heathen?

With ball ammunition
load and lock
load and lock your pieces.

We have our father's work to do.
It says so in the Bible.
Burn their huts and cut them down.
To justice they are liable.

Christ, dear Lord, our hands are red,
red, as with your blood.
But we'll not rest until evil's gone
and all is God's and good.

With ball ammunition
load and lock
load and lock your pieces.

Four Canticles

I

Laws, old before man
and his prating of formula,
guide missles flung from tubes,
to the target-flesh of farmers
tilling in fields a hill away,
beyond herd-sound
and halloo.

II

Programmed with birdlores,
high, the earth is a ball below,
the bombers home on stars
and do not swoop to kill like eagles
but drop fat arrows that know
of vectors, momentums, at when
above the planet to loose their fragments
whirling like dervishes, and mad,
to scythe
the soft men.

III

Before man was man
he weaponed himself
and in the becoming, continued,
weapons his avant-courier,
always ahead and shaping
the new knowings, the new
places
come to.

IV

Our god is a killer god.
Our weapons are more wise
than we, have more will
than we, whom they made.
And shall unmake, if none with plan
arise
in time to tell us how to kill
and still
be man.

Wind Song

I looked into the air and saw a plane
all silver on the sky's gray counterpane.
I heard the dynamed engines, felt them strain
against the leash of earth, and to attain
their black objective, hurling iron rain
on site of hill and town and field and grain,
those dexterous wings of typed and careful brain,
those heaven-high, hell-depth deep sons of Cain.

And often have armadas outward bound
to dump their deadly loads on hill and town
been stung by waspish foemen droning round
and arrows launching upward from the ground.
And often have the bombers vaulted down,
their requiems the wind and cannon sound.

Disquisition
After the Blast

Hey!
Wha - ?

—glad
to taste the wind thresholding April
and to consider that a friend,
while waiting at some windy place,
might also have marvelled and surmised.

V

Our Gods

Odd are our gods,
and arbitrary.
They have our faces,
or the faces
of our fears.

They have our contour,
except for the slave
whose god
is the mold of his master.

Age and legend shape them,
using our hands.

You Don' Worry Me

I don.' worry you
and you don' worry me.
So, what we gonna do?
We gon' leave each other be.
'Cause I don' walk with you
don' mean I walk alone.
Skies can still be blue
even if you ain't my own.

Black Woman

When I see a Black Woman,
Her Blackness positive,
her self, her body, saying
"Yes, it's me!"
I know we are beset
but not besieged.

When I hear a Black Man
applauding a Black Woman,
finding her sweet,
his self's need,
I know that we may ail
but will not die.

Black eases me. Tomorrow
will come from strong loins.
Tomorrow
will be stronger.

Void, Song of

I'll go no more
to the church to pray.
They have empty promise there
and sundown day.

On the Grass

I love you lying
on the grass
a curvature
of tit and ass.

What Are We?

What are we
who call us "Man"
and pride ourselves
that we are plan,
our thinking, "Since we did,
we can"?

Who knows?
The goldfish in his bowl
conceives, perhaps,
his world the whole
and builds ideas
about a soul.

Bar Girl

She has a tremor
in her aft
that makes for
pleasantries to waft
thru the mind,
and provokes philosophy
that mostly men
do not see
much before
but think behind.

Our Children Crying

I hear our children crying
in the buildings
massed like red mesas
on State Street's sunset side,
buildings pocked
with a thousand cavemouths
and old
when they were new.

And even when I cannot hear
our children
yet do I know,
they cry on the Westside,
and in Cleveland,
Belize, Accra, Swaziland,
everywhere
in the world.

Everywhere in the barrens
of sprawled tin
and adobe,
in the buttes of old wood,
of heaped brick, of stone,
and in the concrete piles
pretending
to be new.

Old River

Why should I go then
down to the rim
of Chicago's river?
I cannot bathe myself
in its waters.
I cannot drink.
I cannot wash my clothes there
and dry them in the sun.

Why should I search there
along its banks?
There are no moveable stones.
And muddy shallows are,
even in the deep center
of its stream.
No sea-things meander
the cemented stones.

Why should I hope there,
pause, look for life's leap,
be loathe to come away?
There is no warm suck in
its cold bosom-
only the tired momentums of
old, oil-strangled water.

The Cabbage Worm

The cabbage worm
is green and white.
And why not?
when every bite
of its milieu
is green and white.

New Widow

When his bowels gave way
she knew her old man was dead
and, sighing,
remembered a horse doing that
after being shot in the head.

Closed Systems

This is a thing called, *Grape,*
and this, *Stone,*
or *Now,* or *Night.*
And this is called a *color,*
and this, a *shape.*
Nothing is wrong,
or right.

Me, the green grass,
the names of places,
identities of neighbors.
Me, house, substance, texture.
I do not know.
I do not know.
I live
and I am life.
I die
and I am death.

Whirl

Whirl the wheels madly.
What does it matter?
There is a frantic
in our clatter
and all our ologies
are antic.

H. Rapp Brown

America will never forgive you,
H. Rapp Brown,
for making her Nigras mean.

Two Fables West

See the hero's silver gun
flash, decisive, in the sun
against the bad guy who goes down
to life a legend for the town.

* * *

Guns tied down,
the stinking stranger
untamed and tiger,
is full of danger,
a swagger of jungle,
an aura of anger.
Oh king of the hill,
may you live forever.

Dear Carl

The fog
does not come on
little catfeet
anymore.

Adjust, Adapt

Adjust, Adapt,
twist the gold ring.
God's in his heaven.
It don't mean a thing.

Got a Girl

Motor running,
heart beating,
world turning,
got a girl.
Hot damn!

Murder One in Woodlawn

Who killed these houses,
these places where once
dreams fruited, ripened,
came to pass?

Idea, I say idea
has done them to death.
Their fruit was not meant
to be dreams.

Mortgages, taxes, rents,
was the idea, income
for the building trades,
the developers,
the business-as-usual moles
burrowing, de-rooting, sapping
the ground once sweet.

Only if dreams can flower
from middens, from
a heaped and random compost,
will there be dreams.

Lionlife

Lionlife is not long.
Lions leap
but cannot run
far or fast.
A man is strong
twice as long
as lions live.

Manroar is louder
than lionroar.
Manpaw paces
veldt and meadow
over liondust.
His head too heavy
for hunting,

the lionwoman
pimps her mate.
It is better
to be man
or, seen from lioneyes,
it is fortunate
to be god.

Who Is Captain?

Who is captain with knowledges
of stars
and sense of systems and of suns
to plot and pilot, take command,
and seek the promise of this land?

Through empty places we have come.
Let us listen to the sea-roar
in our bloodbeat and remember.

Who is keen of eye and logical,
has strength
and wit for houses, strength and wit
to curve the light to this dark place
and save our dinosauric race?

Through forms and phyla we have come.
Let us listen to the sea-roar
in our bloodbeat and remember.

Where is the man sane and tall,
and sure
of azimuth? Or is there none,
and we from our own height
must find across the land to light?

Mourning,
sound of a lone thing mourning,
the wind—a grim ghoul mourning
in haunted tune to a gloom
mad moon, lone-thing, wind-sing, mad
mad moon, the wind a grim ghoul,
moon sound, wind-thing, mourning.

Hollow
wind sighing past emptiness
of swept hill, sighing through trees
stricken, stirring dusts that once
tasted the blood of a christ,
wind saying, "My god, My God,
Thou hast forsaken me."

This place
knew day. Summer's rose. Summer's
dawns were here. Bird—flight marked once
its mornings. Noons burned golden in
its summer gleams of sun.
Twilights were a fleeting shade,
soft, and impermanent.

But men
with nails and spears fought the light
and caused Golgotha, bleak,
to loom alone, an empty place
that listens to echoing
cries of a christ echoing
down ages, past a hill.

Come now the Alewives
to lifeless lie in millions
on the beaches.
One cannot but wonder,
while passing by,
at so much death,
and ponder Why?

What minutiae
in the restless water
coalesced
to form such blood and breath?
What wave inane, or mind,
moved those masses
to these shores?

Death Is Not Sleep

Death is not sleep,
nor ending nor beginning.
Yet it is more than
not having been.
Death is life's dime,
tails up.

What If?

What if the atoms of my breath
be galaxies,
and all man's great philosophies
his fear of death?

Windy Place

Gerard Lew had died and against
my press-of-living thoughts, mortgage, job,
Goddamn-car's-in-the-shop-again thoughts,
I remembered talks with him.

The buses were running late that morning.
Good thing it was warmer. The March wind
tasted of April. A car passed,
its wheels flicking a bottle cap on end,
and with the wind the cap was set in motion.

Inevitably thoughts arose on how
a wind from friendly quarter,
exact in time, could so occur
and come about the small erratic shape
and lift it up and make it move.

Flashing, it wheeled the intersection
through traffic mindless and immense
to its own somewhere on the other side,
itself mindless, and perhaps, immense.

What trick of wheel pinching against the pavement
calibrated and caught the unplanned configuration
of its fluted rim, against unlikely chance.
set it upright, chose a horizon, aimed it?

I did not know, but I was glad
to taste the wind thresholding April
and to consider that a friend,
while waiting at some windy place,
might also have marvelled and surmised.

If you like this book . . . **WINDY PLACE**

you will like some of our other books listed on the inside front cover or on our flyers. You can order them conveniently by mailing this order form.

I enclose $_____ for the books listed below. (Add 25 cents for postage and handling.)

Author	Title	Price	No. of Copies	Total

Send me free subscription to Newsletter ☐

Send me free announcements of new books ☐

Postage and Handling _____.25

Grand Total $_____

Name_____

Address_____

City_____State_____Zip_____

Mail check or money order to

BROADSIDE PRESS

Dept. M.O., 12651 Old Mill Place   Detroit, Michigan 48238

71